Beyond the Spotlight

Darren Hayes

Journey of Self-Discovery and
Musical Freedom

John Lucas Whitehead

Beyond the Spotlight

DARREN

HAYES

JOHN LUCAS WHITEHEAD

Table of content

Chapter 1: Early Life and Career Beginnings

Childhood and Early Musical Influences

Darren Stanley Hayes was born on May 8, 1972, in Brisbane, Queensland, Australia. Raised in the working-class suburb of Logan City, Hayes' childhood was far from glamorous, yet it was filled with experiences that shaped the artist he would later become. He grew up as the youngest of three children in a household that, while financially modest, was emotionally rich. His parents, Robert and Judy Hayes, encouraged a love of music in their children, and Darren was no exception. His early exposure to music and his own natural affinity for performance would later serve as the foundation for a career that spanned decades and touched countless lives.

Growing up in Logan City during the 1970s and 1980s was a formative experience for Hayes. His environment was typical of the time, filled with the vibrancy of Australian suburban life but also its challenges. His family's financial struggles were a constant reminder of the harsh realities of working-class life, but it also instilled in him a sense of resilience and determination. While they were not affluent, his parents did their best to provide Darren and his siblings with a stable and loving environment. Music was a constant presence in the household, serving both as a form of escape and emotional expression. Darren himself has remarked in several interviews that his parents often played popular music on the radio, and it was from this that his initial love for the medium grew.

Hayes' childhood was not without its difficulties, though. He has spoken candidly about how being a sensitive child often left him feeling like an outsider, particularly in a culture that tended to prize traditional masculine traits. This sense of isolation, coupled with his family's economic situation, gave him a profound sense of introspection and vulnerability, which would later be a key feature of his songwriting. Despite the challenges, Hayes never felt completely alone, as music became his closest companion during these formative years.

Early Love for Music

From a young age, Darren Hayes showed an intense interest in music and performing. He was particularly drawn to the emotive power of songs and the way music could express feelings that words alone could not. His earliest musical influences included iconic artists like Michael Jackson, Prince, and Madonna, each of whom would later impact his artistic direction in terms of both vocal style and performance. Michael Jackson's Thriller album, in particular, left a lasting impression on Hayes, with its mix of pop, rock, and R&B styles shaping his sense of what modern pop music could be. He would often imitate Jackson's dance moves and sing along to his records, captivated by the combination of emotional depth and high-energy performance that defined Jackson's style. Another key influence was Elton John, whose ability to craft deeply personal songs within the framework of mainstream pop left a mark on Hayes. Elton John's combination of poetic lyrics and melodic complexity resonated with the young Darren, giving him an early appreciation for the power of songwriting. In a similar vein, artists like Prince inspired him with their genre-blurring approach to music, effortlessly combining rock, funk, and pop elements in a way that pushed the boundaries of what pop music could achieve.

Madonna's boundary-pushing performances and reinventions over the years provided Hayes with a template for how an artist could continuously evolve while remaining true to their artistic core. Her boldness in exploring themes of identity, love, and sexuality also played a crucial role in shaping Hayes' understanding of how music could serve as a platform for self-expression and social commentary. These early influences would come to define much of Hayes' career, from his work with Savage Garden to his later solo endeavors.

Discovering His Voice

While Darren Hayes always had an innate love for music, it wasn't until his teenage years that he began to explore his own voice. Singing became a way for him to express the complex emotions he often found difficult to articulate otherwise. He found solace in performing, first to himself and later to friends and family. In his early teens, Hayes was already trying to mimic the vocal acrobatics of his idols. His voice, which would later be praised for its wide range and emotive power, was still developing, but even at this stage, it was clear that Hayes had a gift.

During his time at Mabel Park High School, Hayes became involved in school plays and musicals, which offered him his first real taste of performing in front of an audience. His participation in school productions allowed him to build confidence in his voice and stage presence. These early experiences were crucial in helping Hayes understand the unique blend of vulnerability and strength required to be a successful performer.

At this stage, music was more of a passion than a career aspiration. Though Hayes loved to perform, the idea of pursuing music professionally seemed far-fetched given his background. His initial plan was to become a teacher, and he even enrolled in a teaching course at the University of Queensland after high school. However, his love for music never waned, and fate had other plans.

The Role of 1980s Pop Culture

The cultural landscape of the 1980s had a profound effect on Darren Hayes, as it did on countless artists of his generation. It was a time when pop music was undergoing a transformation, with MTV emerging as a dominant force in shaping musical trends and artist personas. Visual presentation became just as important as the music itself, and artists like Michael Jackson, Madonna, and Prince mastered the art of combining music with performance and video to create an all-encompassing experience for their audience.

Hayes was fascinated by this aspect of the music industry. The flamboyance and theatricality of pop music in the 1980s gave him permission to dream of a future where he could combine his love for music with his natural flair for drama. He became particularly enamored with the idea of storytelling through music videos, a concept that would later influence his own artistic output.

The rise of electronic music and synthesizers also left a significant mark on Hayes. Bands like Depeche Mode and Eurythmics, who blended electronic sounds with emotional depth, became important touchstones for him. The use of electronic instruments to convey emotion fascinated Hayes, and this would later be a hallmark of his work, particularly in his solo career where he experimented more freely with electronic sounds and production techniques.

First Steps into Songwriting

As Darren Hayes' passion for music deepened, he began to explore songwriting. Initially, this was more of a hobby than a serious pursuit. However, as he experimented with melodies and lyrics, he began to realize that songwriting offered him a way to process his emotions and experiences. In many ways, songwriting became a form of therapy for Hayes, allowing him to channel his feelings of isolation, longing, and hope into something creative and tangible.

Hayes has often spoken about the cathartic power of music and how writing songs allowed him to express feelings he struggled to communicate in other ways. His lyrics, even in these early stages, were introspective and deeply personal, often dealing with themes of love, identity, and emotional vulnerability. This would become a defining characteristic of his work throughout his career.

His early songs were rough and unpolished, but they provided the foundation for what would later become a signature style: emotionally charged lyrics paired with memorable melodies. As he continued to write and refine his craft, Hayes began to see music not just as a passion, but as a potential career path. The more he immersed himself in songwriting, the more he realized that he had something unique to offer the world.

The Beginnings of a Dream

By the time Darren Hayes reached his late teens, it was clear that music was more than just a passing interest. His talent was undeniable, and his passion for performing and songwriting only grew stronger with time. Although the path to a successful music career seemed daunting, especially for a young man from a working-class suburb, Hayes was determined to follow his dream.

His early musical influences, combined with his natural talent and emotional sensitivity, set the stage for what would become an extraordinary career. Darren Hayes may have been a small-town boy from Logan City, but his ambitions and talents were far larger than the confines of his upbringing. Little did he know that his journey was only just beginning, and that he was on the verge of a breakthrough that would catapult him to international stardom.

These early experiences would serve as the bedrock for his future success, shaping not only the kind of artist he would become but also the themes and emotions he would explore in his music. From a young age, Darren Hayes knew that music was his calling, and he was willing to follow that calling wherever it led him.

Formation and Success of Savage Garden

The Birth of Savage Garden

The formation of Savage Garden marked a pivotal moment in Darren Hayes' career, one that catapulted him from relative obscurity to international stardom. Savage Garden, an Australian pop duo, was formed in 1993 when Hayes teamed up with multi-instrumentalist and composer Daniel Jones. The duo would go on to become one of the most successful and influential pop acts of the late 1990s, known for their emotive lyrics, polished production, and timeless melodies.

Meeting Daniel Jones

The story of Savage Garden begins with a fortuitous meeting between Darren Hayes and Daniel Jones. Jones, a talented musician who was part of a Brisbane band called Red Edge, had posted an advertisement in a local music publication, seeking a lead singer. Hayes, then a student at the University of Queensland, saw the ad and decided to audition. At the time, Hayes was still unsure of his future in music and had only dabbled in singing and songwriting. However, he had a deep desire to express himself through music and saw the audition as a potential opportunity.

The chemistry between Hayes and Jones was instantaneous. While Jones was impressed with Hayes' vocal range and emotive delivery, Hayes was equally captivated by Jones' skill as a composer and instrumentalist. The two shared a love for similar musical genres and artists, from pop icons like Michael Jackson and Madonna to the sophisticated sounds of bands like U2 and Depeche Mode. They quickly discovered that their creative visions aligned, and this mutual understanding laid the foundation for a fruitful partnership.

In 1994, Red Edge disbanded, and Hayes and Jones decided to form their own group. The duo initially called themselves Crush, but soon changed their name to Savage Garden, inspired by a phrase from Anne Rice's novel The Vampire Chronicles, where the "savage garden" represented the chaotic and predatory nature of the world. This name resonated with both of them, capturing the intensity and passion they hoped to convey through their music.

Early Struggles and Breakthroughs

The early days of Savage Garden were characterized by hard work and perseverance. Hayes and Jones dedicated themselves to writing songs and honing their sound. They rented a small studio in Brisbane where they worked tirelessly, often staying up late into the night to perfect their music. Both artists were committed to creating something unique, blending elements of pop, rock, and electronic music to craft a sound that was both modern and timeless.

One of the first songs they wrote together was "A Thousand Words," a track that demonstrated their ability to merge catchy pop hooks with deeply emotional lyrics. Although they had little experience in the music industry at this stage, they believed in their material and were determined to make it.

Their big break came when they submitted a demo tape to John Woodruff, an Australian music manager who had previously worked with artists like Baby Animals and Noiseworks. Woodruff was immediately impressed by their potential and agreed to manage them. He sent their demo to several record labels, and after receiving multiple rejections, Savage Garden was eventually signed to Roadshow Music in Australia.

In 1996, Savage Garden released their debut single, "I Want You," which quickly became a hit. The song's infectious energy, Hayes' smooth vocals, and its catchy chorus made it a standout on Australian radio. "I Want You" reached number four on the Australian ARIA Singles Chart and garnered attention from international markets. The success of the single led to a deal with Columbia Records, and soon Savage Garden was poised to break into the global music scene.

Self-Titled Debut Album

Savage Garden's self-titled debut album, released in March 1997, was a commercial and critical success. The album showcased Darren Hayes' distinctive vocals and Daniel Jones' sophisticated production, blending pop, rock, and electronic influences into a cohesive and innovative sound. The album was meticulously crafted, with both Hayes and Jones playing a central role in its production and creative direction.

The album produced a string of hit singles, each of which demonstrated the duo's versatility and ability to connect with audiences on an emotional level. "I Want You," with its fast-paced, almost frenetic energy, became a radio staple. The track featured rapid-fire lyrics and an infectious chorus, setting the stage for Savage Garden's rise to international fame.

Their second single, "To the Moon and Back," showcased a more introspective side of Savage Garden. The song, which dealt with themes of isolation and yearning for love, resonated with listeners, climbing the charts in several countries. It was particularly successful in the United Kingdom, where it reached the top three on the UK Singles Chart.

However, it was their third single, "Truly Madly Deeply," that truly cemented Savage Garden's place in pop history. The ballad, with its heartfelt lyrics and tender melody, became an anthem of love and devotion. "Truly Madly Deeply" topped the charts in multiple countries, including the United States, where it spent two weeks at number one on the Billboard Hot 100. The song's universal appeal made it one of the most enduring hits of the 1990s, and it remains one of Savage Garden's signature tracks.

The success of these singles catapulted the Savage Garden album to the top of the charts. The album sold millions of copies worldwide and established Hayes and Jones as one of the most successful musical duos of the late 1990s. Their unique ability to combine catchy melodies with emotionally resonant lyrics set them apart from their contemporaries, earning them both critical and commercial acclaim.

International Stardom

With the success of their debut album, Savage Garden quickly became an international sensation. Darren Hayes, in particular, was thrust into the spotlight, with his charismatic stage presence and emotive vocal performances captivating audiences around the world. The duo embarked on a world tour, performing to sold-out crowds in Europe, North America, and Asia.

The global success of Savage Garden was unprecedented for an Australian act at the time. Their music transcended geographic boundaries, appealing to a wide range of listeners with its universal themes of love, longing, and self-discovery. Hayes' voice, often described as haunting and ethereal, became synonymous with the band's sound, while Jones' instrumental prowess and production skills added a layer of sophistication to their recordings.

One of the defining features of Savage Garden's music was its emotional accessibility. Hayes and Jones crafted songs that were not only radio-friendly but also deeply personal. Darren Hayes' lyrics often explored themes of love, identity, and vulnerability, resonating with listeners on a profound level. Whether through upbeat anthems like "I Want You" or tender ballads like "Truly Madly Deeply," Savage Garden had an uncanny ability to tap into the emotional core of their audience.

Accolades and Awards

As their popularity grew, so too did the accolades. Savage Garden was showered with numerous awards and honors for their contributions to pop music. At the 1997 ARIA Music Awards, they won a record-breaking ten awards, including Best Group, Album of the Year (Savage Garden), and Single of the Year ("Truly Madly Deeply"). These accolades were a testament to their impact on the Australian music scene, as well as their growing international influence.

The band's success was not limited to Australia, however. In the United States, they were nominated for several Billboard Music Awards, including Top Hot 100 Artist and Top Pop Artist. In the UK, they received nominations for BRIT Awards and MTV Europe Music Awards. Their ability to connect with audiences across different cultures and demographics made them one of the most successful global pop acts of the late 1990s.

Sophomore Success: Affirmation

In 1999, Savage Garden released their second and final studio album, Affirmation. The album marked a stylistic shift for the duo, with a more polished and mature sound. The themes explored on Affirmation were deeper and more introspective, reflecting the personal growth that both Hayes and Jones had experienced since the release of their debut album.

The lead single, "The Animal Song," was an energetic, upbeat track that celebrated the joys of living life to the fullest. It was a commercial success, reaching the top of the charts in several countries. However, it was the album's second single, "I Knew I Loved You," that became one of the band's biggest hits. The romantic ballad, reminiscent of "Truly Madly Deeply," topped the Billboard Hot 100 chart for four weeks, further cementing Savage Garden's place in pop music history.

Other standout tracks from Affirmation included the title track, which explored themes of self-acceptance and personal growth, and "Crash and Burn," a song about supporting loved ones through difficult times. The album resonated with both critics and fans, and it went on to sell millions of copies worldwide.

The End of Savage Garden

Despite their continued success, tensions began to emerge within the duo. Darren Hayes and Daniel Jones had different visions for the future of Savage Garden, and their partnership began to fray. Jones, who had always been more interested in the production and behind-the-scenes aspects of music, grew increasingly weary of the pressures of fame and touring. Hayes, on the other hand, had developed a passion for performing and songwriting and wanted to continue pushing the band's creative boundaries.

In 2001, Savage Garden officially disbanded. The news came as a shock to their fans, who had hoped for more music from the duo. However, both Hayes and Jones expressed gratitude for their time together and pride in what they had achieved. Savage Garden's brief but brilliant career left an indelible mark on the pop music landscape, and their music continues to be celebrated by fans around the world.

For Darren Hayes, the end of Savage Garden marked the beginning of a new chapter in his musical journey.

He would go on to pursue a successful solo career, releasing several critically acclaimed albums and continuing to evolve as an artist. Daniel Jones, meanwhile, stepped away from the spotlight and focused on other ventures, including music production

Chapter 2: Solo Debut and Rise to Fame

The Release of *Spin* (2002)

The release of Darren Hayes' solo debut album, Spin, in 2002 was a significant moment in his career, marking the transition from his celebrated work with Savage Garden to a solo artist seeking to carve out a new identity in the music industry. After the disbandment of Savage Garden in 2001, Hayes faced both anticipation and skepticism as fans and critics wondered whether he could replicate the success of his former band. Spin was Hayes' response to these expectations, a record that showcased his personal growth, musical evolution, and desire to break free from the pop formula that had characterized Savage Garden's greatest hits.

The Creative Process Behind Spin
For Spin, Hayes worked with renowned producer Walter Afanasieff, known for his collaborations with

artists like Mariah Carey, Celine Dion, and Whitney Houston. Afanasieff was a natural choice for Hayes, as he shared his passion for creating lush, sophisticated pop music with emotional depth. Together, they crafted a record that was a departure from the sound of Savage Garden, blending pop with R&B, electronic, and even dance influences. The collaboration was a deliberate attempt by Hayes to broaden his musical palette and experiment with new styles while maintaining his signature melodic sensibilities.

Hayes took an active role in the songwriting and production process, ensuring that Spin reflected his personal experiences and artistic vision. Whereas Savage Garden's songs had been co-written with Daniel Jones, Spin was entirely Hayes' project. The album's lyrics delved into more mature themes of love, heartbreak, self-identity, and personal reflection, signaling Hayes' desire to establish himself as a solo artist with his own voice. The emotional depth of the lyrics, combined with the album's slick production, created a record that was both introspective and accessible to a broad audience.

In many ways, Spin was an album about transformation. For Hayes, it represented a chance to reinvent himself after the dissolution of Savage Garden, to step out of the shadow of his past success, and to explore new musical territories. At the same time, the album carried the weight of expectation—both from the industry and from Hayes himself, who wanted to prove that he could succeed on his own terms.

The Lead Single: "Insatiable"

The first single from Spin was "Insatiable," a sensual, slow-burning ballad that immediately set the tone for the album. Released in January 2002, "Insatiable" was a significant departure from the upbeat, radio-friendly pop hits that had made Savage Garden famous. The song's sultry vibe, atmospheric production, and Hayes' breathy, intimate vocal delivery were strikingly different from anything he had done before. Lyrically, the song dealt with themes of desire and yearning, showcasing Hayes' ability to craft deeply emotional and personal narratives within his music.

"Insatiable" was not only a bold choice for a lead single but also a statement of intent: Hayes was no longer part of a pop duo; he was now a solo artist capable of exploring more adult and complex themes. The song received a mixed initial reaction from critics, some of whom praised its lush production and Hayes' vocal performance, while others felt it lacked the immediacy of Savage Garden's hits. However, the song's success on the charts—reaching the top 10 in Australia, the UK, and several other countries—proved that Hayes' new direction resonated with a global audience.

Chart Success and Critical Reception of Spin

Spin was officially released on March 18, 2002, and was met with a strong commercial response, particularly in Australia and the United Kingdom. The album debuted at number two on the Australian Albums Chart and number three on the UK Albums Chart, establishing Hayes as a formidable solo artist in his home country and abroad. The record's chart performance demonstrated that Hayes had successfully navigated the transition from being one-half of a duo to standing alone as a solo performer.

Global Chart Performance

While Spin was especially successful in Australia and the UK, it also performed well in other markets, including Europe and parts of Asia. In the United States, however, the album did not achieve the same level of commercial success as Savage Garden's releases. It peaked at number 35 on the Billboard 200 chart, which was a respectable showing but fell short of the massive impact Savage Garden had previously made on the American charts. Despite this, Spin sold over two million copies worldwide, solidifying Hayes' position as an international pop star.

The success of Spin can be attributed in part to its well-crafted, radio-friendly singles, which resonated with fans who had followed Hayes from his Savage Garden days. In addition to "Insatiable," other tracks such as "Strange Relationship" and "Crush (1980 Me)" were released as singles, each contributing to the album's continued presence on the charts. "Strange Relationship," with its upbeat tempo and catchy chorus, became a fan favorite and highlighted Hayes' ability to blend introspective lyrics with infectious melodies. "Crush (1980 Me)," a nostalgic ode to 1980s pop culture, further showcased Hayes' versatility as a songwriter and performer, blending fun, playful elements with more serious undertones.

Critical Reception

The critical reception of Spin was generally positive, with many reviewers praising Hayes' vocal abilities and the album's polished production. Critics noted that Hayes had matured as an artist, moving beyond the commercial pop sound that had defined his work with Savage Garden and embracing a more nuanced and emotionally rich approach. However, some critics were less enthusiastic about the album's stylistic shift, feeling that Spin lacked the immediacy and energy of his earlier work.

In particular, Hayes' collaboration with Walter Afanasieff was singled out for praise. Afanasieff's production gave the album a smooth, sophisticated sound that complemented Hayes' emotive vocals. Songs like "Insatiable" and "I Miss You" were noted for their lush arrangements and attention to detail, while tracks like "Dirty" and "Good Enough" revealed Hayes' willingness to experiment with different genres and push the boundaries of his pop sensibilities.

Though some critics argued that Spin was too polished and lacked the raw emotional intensity of Savage Garden's best work, most agreed that Hayes had successfully established himself as a solo artist capable of delivering both commercial hits and more introspective, personal material. The album's success affirmed Hayes' place in the pop landscape and demonstrated that he had the ability to evolve as an artist while staying true to his unique voice.

Touring and Promotion for Spin

The release of Spin was followed by an extensive promotional campaign, including a world tour that saw Darren Hayes performing in venues across Europe, Asia, and Australia. Hayes embraced the opportunity to connect with his fans as a solo artist and was determined to prove that he could command the stage on his own, without the backing of a band or a partner. The Spin tour marked a significant moment in Hayes' career, as it allowed him to establish a personal connection with his audience and showcase his growth as a performer.

The Spin Tour

The Spin tour kicked off in April 2002, with dates in the United Kingdom and Europe, before moving on to Australia and Asia. Although the tour did not extend to the United States, it was a major success in other markets, with Hayes performing to sold-out crowds in major cities such as London, Paris, Sydney, and Tokyo. The setlist for the tour included a mix of songs from Spin and select Savage Garden hits, allowing Hayes to bridge the gap between his past and present. One of the highlights of the tour was Hayes' vocal performance, which was widely praised for its emotional depth and technical precision. Throughout the shows, Hayes delivered impassioned renditions of songs like "Insatiable" and "I Miss You," demonstrating his ability to convey vulnerability and longing in his music. He also incorporated more upbeat numbers like "Crush (1980 Me)" and "Strange Relationship" into the setlist, ensuring that the energy remained high throughout the concerts.

The Spin tour was also an opportunity for Hayes to experiment with his live performances. Unlike the large-scale, highly produced Savage Garden shows, which had relied heavily on elaborate stage designs and visual effects, the Spin concerts were more intimate and focused on Hayes' connection with the audience. He often engaged in candid conversations with fans between songs, sharing personal stories and insights into his songwriting process. This level of openness helped to endear Hayes to his audience, further solidifying his reputation as an artist who was willing to be vulnerable and authentic in his music.

Television and Media Appearances
In addition to touring, Hayes also made numerous television appearances to promote Spin, both in

Australia and internationally. He performed on popular talk shows and music programs, including Top of the Pops, MTV, and The Tonight Show with Jay Leno, where he delivered live performances of singles like "Insatiable" and "Strange Relationship." These performances helped to boost the album's visibility and further established Hayes as a solo artist in the public eye.

Hayes' media appearances were often accompanied by interviews in which he discussed his decision to pursue a solo career, the creative process behind Spin, and his experiences in the music industry. In these interviews, Hayes was candid about the challenges he faced in transitioning from Savage Garden to a solo artist, but he also expressed his excitement about the new direction his music was taking. He spoke openly about the personal themes that informed the album, from his experiences with love and heartbreak to his reflections on identity and self-acceptance.

Fan Engagement

One of the key factors in Hayes' success during this period was his ability to maintain a close connection with his fanbase. He was active on social media and often engaged with fans through online forums and fan sites, where he shared updates about the album and tour. Hayes' openness and accessibility endeared him to his fans, many of whom had followed him since his days in Savage Garden. His willingness to share his personal journey and creative process made him a relatable and beloved figure among his supporters.

Darren Hayes' solo debut with Spin marked the beginning of a new chapter in his career, as he successfully transitioned from being part of one of the most successful pop duos of the 1990s to standing on his own as a solo artist. The release of Spin, its chart success, and the extensive touring and promotion that followed solidified Hayes' position as a versatile and talented performer. The album allowed him to explore new musical styles and themes, while also maintaining the emotional depth and lyrical intimacy that had made Savage Garden so beloved.

Chapter 3: Creative Evolution in *The Tension and the Spark*

Released in 2004, Darren Hayes' second solo album, The Tension and the Spark, marked a profound transformation in his career. Unlike his debut album, Spin (2002), which had focused on more mainstream pop sounds, The Tension and the Spark was a bold experiment that showcased Hayes' growing confidence as a solo artist. The album represented a significant departure from his previous work, with a focus on darker, more introspective themes and a move towards electronic music. This shift not only highlighted Hayes' versatility as an artist but also underscored his willingness to take creative risks and push the boundaries of pop music.

Musical Shift and Experimentation

One of the most striking aspects of The Tension and the Spark was its dramatic musical shift. While Hayes had already demonstrated his pop prowess with Savage Garden and his solo debut, this album saw him veering away from the polished, radio-friendly sound that had previously defined his career. Instead, Hayes embraced electronic and experimental music, blending synth-pop, ambient, and darker tones to create a sonic landscape that was both innovative and unexpected.

Influence of Electronic and Synth-Pop

At the heart of The Tension and the Spark was its use of electronic production, which represented a significant departure from the guitar-driven pop of Hayes' earlier work. Drawing inspiration from artists like Depeche Mode, Björk, and Trent Reznor of Nine Inch Nails, Hayes created an album that was characterized by moody synths, atmospheric soundscapes, and minimalistic beats. This shift in sound allowed Hayes to explore new ways of expressing himself, using the mechanical and cold qualities of electronic music to underscore the album's themes of alienation, emotional turmoil, and self-discovery.

The album was produced by Hayes alongside Swedish producer Robert Conley, who had a background in electronic music. Together, they crafted a record that was raw, edgy, and highly textured. Hayes used electronic instruments and programming to create a sense of tension throughout the album, with tracks that oscillated between moments of stark minimalism and sweeping, cinematic arrangements. This contrast mirrored the album's thematic focus on inner conflict and the struggle for self-acceptance.

Songs like "Darkness" and "Unlovable" exemplified Hayes' new direction, with haunting synths and brooding lyrics that expressed feelings of insecurity, vulnerability, and isolation. The electronic beats and layered production gave the songs a futuristic and otherworldly quality, creating a sonic environment that felt distant from the warm, acoustic-based sound of Spin. Hayes' experimentation with electronica also allowed him to tap into a more avant-garde and experimental approach to songwriting, eschewing conventional pop structures in favor of a more free-form, abstract style.

Vocal Experimentation

In addition to the musical shift, Hayes also experimented with his vocal delivery on The Tension and the Spark. Known for his powerful, emotive voice, Hayes opted for a more restrained and often understated vocal performance on this album. His voice was frequently processed with effects, including reverb and distortion, giving it a detached and robotic quality that matched the cold, electronic instrumentation. In some songs, Hayes' vocals were layered and manipulated to sound fragmented or distant, further enhancing the themes of disconnection and inner turmoil.

For instance, in the track "Dublin Sky," Hayes' voice alternates between soft, introspective verses and more soaring, emotional choruses, reflecting the tension between vulnerability and strength that runs throughout the album. On "Void," his vocals are deliberately distorted and layered over industrial beats, creating a sense of emotional numbness and alienation. This vocal experimentation was a testament to Hayes' desire to challenge himself artistically and explore new ways of using his voice as an instrument to convey emotion.

Themes of The Tension and the Spark

The Tension and the Spark was not only a musical evolution for Darren Hayes but also a deeply personal exploration of his internal struggles. The album delved into themes of self-doubt, emotional conflict, identity, and the quest for self-acceptance. While Savage Garden's music and Spin had often centered on themes of love and relationships, The Tension and the Spark was far more introspective and existential, reflecting Hayes' personal journey at a pivotal point in his life.

Inner Conflict and Emotional Vulnerability

The central theme of The Tension and the Spark was the tension between light and dark, between hope and despair, and between self-love and self-loathing. Hayes has described the album as being about his own internal battles, and this is evident in the lyrics, which are filled with raw and unfiltered expressions of vulnerability, fear, and uncertainty. The opening track, "Darkness," sets the tone for the album, with its stark, minimalist arrangement and lyrics that explore feelings of insecurity and emotional isolation. Hayes sings about being "afraid to be alone," capturing the fear of confronting one's inner demons.

Throughout the album, Hayes grapples with questions of self-worth and the need for external validation. In songs like "Unlovable," he confronts his feelings of inadequacy and the belief that he is unworthy of love and acceptance. The track's haunting lyrics, "I'm unlovable, you don't love me at all," reflect Hayes' struggle with self-doubt and his desire to be loved despite his perceived flaws. This theme of emotional vulnerability runs throughout the album, with Hayes opening up about his insecurities in a way that feels both cathartic and deeply relatable.

Self-Discovery and Acceptance

While The Tension and the Spark is filled with moments of darkness and despair, it is also an album about self-discovery and the journey towards acceptance. In tracks like "Void" and "Sense of Humor," Hayes explores the idea of confronting one's fears and embracing imperfection. "Void" is a stark meditation on the emptiness and numbness that can come from emotional detachment, but it also suggests the possibility of breaking free from that void and finding a sense of purpose. Similarly, "Sense of Humor" is a more lighthearted track that encourages self-compassion and the ability to laugh at one's mistakes.

The album's title, The Tension and the Spark, reflects the duality at the heart of the record—the tension between despair and hope, between self-criticism and self-acceptance, and between fear and courage. Hayes has spoken about how the album was a way for him to process his own emotional struggles and come to terms with his identity. The "spark" in the title represents the moments of clarity and inspiration that can emerge from even the darkest periods of introspection.

Exploration of Identity and Sexuality

Another important theme in The Tension and the Spark is Hayes' exploration of identity, including his sexuality. Although Hayes had not publicly come out as gay at the time of the album's release, many of the songs on the record reflect his journey of self-acceptance and the struggle to reconcile his true self with societal expectations. Tracks like "Hero" and "Ego" hint at the pressures Hayes faced in maintaining a public persona while grappling with his personal identity. The lyrics of "Hero" reflect the desire to break free from the expectations placed on him by others, while "Ego" addresses the masks people wear to hide their insecurities.

Though The Tension and the Spark does not explicitly deal with issues of sexuality, the album's themes of self-acceptance and identity resonate with Hayes' later decision to come out publicly. The album can be seen as a precursor to Hayes' more open discussion of his sexuality in his subsequent work, as well as a reflection of the internal struggles he faced during this period of his life.

Reception and Impact of the Album

When The Tension and the Spark was released in 2004, it was met with a mixed reaction from both fans and critics. While some praised Hayes' willingness to experiment and embrace a darker, more electronic sound, others were taken aback by the album's departure from his earlier, more accessible pop material. However, over time, the album has come to be seen as one of Hayes' most important and innovative works, both for its bold musical direction and its deeply personal themes.

Critical Reception

Critically, The Tension and the Spark received praise for its emotional depth and musical experimentation. Many reviewers highlighted Hayes' growth as an artist, noting that the album's darker and more introspective themes represented a significant evolution from the more straightforward pop of Spin. The production, which combined electronic elements with Hayes' signature emotive vocals, was also praised for its originality and sophistication.

However, not all reviews were positive. Some critics felt that the album's experimental nature made it less accessible to a mainstream audience, particularly those who had followed Hayes from his Savage Garden days. The album's heavy use of electronic production and its introspective, sometimes melancholic themes were a stark contrast to the more commercial sound of Hayes' previous work, and some fans found it challenging to connect with.

Commercial Performance

Commercially, The Tension and the Spark did not achieve the same level of success as Hayes' debut solo album. While Spin had been a commercial hit, especially in the UK and Australia, The Tension and the Spark struggled to match its predecessor's sales. The lead single, "Pop!ular," was a moderate success, reaching the top 10 in the UK and Australia, but the album as a whole did not perform as well on the charts.

Despite its commercial underperformance, The Tension and the Spark has since gained a cult following and is regarded by many fans as one of

Hayes' most important and influential works. The album's introspective themes and bold musical experimentation have earned it a lasting legacy, and it is often cited as a turning point in Hayes' career, representing his willingness to take creative risks and push the boundaries of pop music.

Legacy and Influence

In the years since its release, The Tension and the Spark has been recognized as a pivotal album in Darren Hayes' discography. While it may not have achieved the same commercial success as some of his other works, it has had a lasting impact on his career and on the broader pop music landscape. The album's exploration of electronic music and its dark, introspective themes helped pave the way for other pop artists who sought to blend mainstream pop with more experimental and avant-garde influences.

Moreover, The Tension and the Spark represents a significant moment in Hayes' personal and artistic journey. It was during this period that he began to come to terms with his identity, and the album's themes of self-discovery and emotional vulnerability reflect the challenges he faced as he navigated this process. For many fans, the album resonates on a deeply personal level, offering a raw and honest reflection of the complexities of the human experience.

The Tension and the Spark was a bold and transformative album for Darren Hayes. Its musical shift towards electronic experimentation, combined with its deeply personal and introspective themes, represented a significant evolution in Hayes' career. While the album may not have achieved the same commercial success as some of his earlier work, it remains one of his most critically acclaimed and artistically ambitious projects. The Tension and the Spark stands as a testament to Hayes' willingness to take creative risks and push the boundaries of pop music, solidifying his place as a unique and visionary artist in the pop world.

Chapter 4: Independent Releases and Artistic Freedom

After the initial success of his solo albums and the challenges that followed, Darren Hayes embarked on a journey that allowed him to fully express his creative vision. This period marked a significant evolution in his career, characterized by newfound artistic freedom and a commitment to authenticity. Hayes' decision to operate independently enabled him to take control of his music, explore innovative ideas, and redefine his identity as an artist. This chapter delves into Hayes' independent releases, highlighting his establishment of Powdered Sugar, the release of This Delicate Thing We've Made, and the collaborative album We Are Smug.

Founding Powdered Sugar: A New Path

In the wake of The Tension and the Spark, Darren Hayes made the pivotal decision to part ways with major record labels and establish his own independent label, Powdered Sugar. This move was driven by a desire for creative autonomy, as Hayes sought to reclaim control over his music and the artistic process. By founding Powdered Sugar, he aimed to create a platform that would allow him to explore his musical ideas without the constraints imposed by the commercial music industry.

Motivation for Independence

Hayes' motivation for becoming an independent artist stemmed from his experiences within the music industry, where he often felt restricted by commercial expectations and the pressures of radio-friendly sound. He was eager to create music that was true to his artistic vision, rather than conforming to the trends and formulas dictated by record labels. The establishment of Powdered Sugar provided Hayes with the opportunity to make music on his own terms, allowing him to experiment freely and delve into personal themes without compromise.

In interviews, Hayes expressed a desire to focus on the artistry rather than the business side of music. He believed that independence would not only enable him to create authentic work but also foster a deeper connection with his audience. By bypassing traditional distribution channels, Hayes aimed to engage with his fans more directly, sharing his music in a way that felt genuine and meaningful.

The First Steps

As part of his new independent journey, Hayes began to explore various musical avenues, including collaborations with other artists and producers. The Powdered Sugar label was not just a means for Hayes to release his music; it also represented a community of creative individuals dedicated to exploring new ideas and pushing artistic boundaries. Hayes began to build a network of collaborators and musicians, all eager to participate in the innovative spirit of Powdered Sugar.

In 2007, Hayes announced that he would be releasing a new album, This Delicate Thing We've Made, under the Powdered Sugar label, signaling the start of a new chapter in his career. The formation of Powdered Sugar not only marked a shift in Hayes' business approach but also a significant transformation in his artistic identity.

This Delicate Thing We've Made (2007)

This Delicate Thing We've Made, released in 2007, was the first full-length album to emerge from Hayes' independent label, Powdered Sugar. The album was a reflection of Hayes' creative evolution and represented a departure from the conventional pop sound that had characterized his earlier work. It showcased his commitment to artistry and authenticity, encapsulating his journey toward self-discovery and artistic freedom.

Concept and Themes

The album is a concept piece, weaving together various themes of love, loss, identity, and personal reflection. It reflects Hayes' experiences since the release of The Tension and the Spark and showcases his growth as both a songwriter and a storyteller. The lyrics delve into the complexities of human relationships, examining both the joyous and painful moments that define love and connection. In songs like "Step into the Light" and "The Only One," Hayes explores the challenges of vulnerability and the desire for acceptance.

This Delicate Thing We've Made also features a strong thematic focus on the passage of time and the impact of memories. Hayes often reflects on his past, pondering how experiences shape our identities and the way we relate to one another. Tracks like "Who Would Have Thought" illustrate this introspective journey, as Hayes grapples with the unpredictability of life and the notion of fate.

Musical Style and Experimentation
Musically, This Delicate Thing We've Made represents a significant departure from Hayes' earlier sound,

incorporating elements of electronic, pop, rock, and orchestral arrangements. The album was produced by Hayes in collaboration with a variety of musicians and producers, leading to a rich and diverse sonic palette. The use of lush strings, synths, and intricate harmonies creates a cinematic quality that complements the emotional depth of the lyrics.

Tracks like "On the Verge of Something Wonderful" and "The Universe" showcase Hayes' ability to blend genres seamlessly, combining catchy pop hooks with experimental sounds and arrangements. The album's production also reflects Hayes' commitment to artistic exploration, as he employed unconventional song structures and layered instrumentation to create a unique listening experience.

One of the standout features of the album is Hayes' vocal performance. His voice shines throughout, with moments of soaring melodies and delicate nuances that convey a wide range of emotions. Hayes' ability to convey vulnerability and strength in his vocals adds depth to the album, allowing listeners to connect with the emotional weight of the songs.

Reception and Impact

Upon its release, This Delicate Thing We've Made received a mixed reception from critics, with some praising its ambitious scope and artistic vision, while others expressed concerns about its departure from the mainstream sound. However, the album garnered a devoted fanbase and solidified Hayes' reputation as an artist willing to take risks and pursue his creative vision.

Despite its mixed critical response, the album achieved moderate commercial success, especially in Australia and the UK. The lead single, "Step into the Light," received positive reviews and gained traction on radio, showcasing Hayes' continued ability to create compelling pop music. The album's themes of self-discovery and emotional honesty resonated with listeners, further deepening Hayes' connection with his audience.

In retrospect, This Delicate Thing We've Made has been regarded as a pivotal work in Hayes' discography. It marked a significant step in his artistic evolution, illustrating his commitment to authenticity and self-exploration. The album's impact extended beyond its initial release, influencing Hayes' subsequent projects and shaping his approach to music-making in the years to come.

Collaborative Album: We Are Smug

Following the release of This Delicate Thing We've Made, Darren Hayes embarked on a collaborative project with his long-time friend and musical partner, Robert Conley. The result of their collaboration was the album We Are Smug, released in 2010. This project further emphasized Hayes' dedication to artistic freedom and the exploration of new musical territories.

Concept and Collaboration

We Are Smug was born out of Hayes' desire to create music in a more relaxed and informal setting. The album was produced in collaboration with Conley and was characterized by a less structured approach compared to Hayes' previous solo efforts. The duo aimed to capture the spontaneity of their creative process, resulting in a collection of songs that felt organic and unfiltered.

The title We Are Smug reflects the playful nature of the project, encapsulating the camaraderie and joy that Hayes and Conley shared during the recording process. The album was not intended to be a major commercial release but rather a fun and artistic endeavor that allowed them to experiment with new sounds and ideas.

Musical Style and Diversity

Musically, We Are Smug is a blend of various genres, incorporating elements of pop, rock, and electronica. The album showcases Hayes' versatility as a vocalist and songwriter, with tracks ranging from upbeat and catchy tunes to introspective ballads. The collaborative nature of the project allowed for a diverse array of influences to come into play, resulting in a rich and eclectic sound.

Songs like "Sing" and "We're Smug" exhibit Hayes' knack for crafting infectious melodies, while tracks such as "Nightswimming" and "I'm Not the One" delve into more reflective and emotional territory. The production style of We Are Smug is characterized by a lo-fi aesthetic, with Hayes and Conley opting for raw, unpolished sounds that capture the authenticity of their collaboration.

Reception and Legacy

We Are Smug received a positive response from fans and critics alike, praised for its playful and experimental approach. While it did not achieve the same level of commercial success as Hayes' previous albums, it further solidified his reputation as an artist unafraid to explore new musical avenues. The album was celebrated for its authenticity and the sense of joy that permeated the recording process.

In retrospect, We Are Smug represents a significant moment in Hayes' artistic journey, showcasing his willingness to embrace collaboration and explore new ideas outside the confines of traditional album releases. The project served as a testament to Hayes' commitment to artistic freedom and his dedication to creating music that reflects his true self.

Darren Hayes' independent releases, including This Delicate Thing We've Made and We Are Smug, marked a turning point in his career, allowing him to fully embrace his artistic freedom and explore new musical territories. The establishment of his label, Powdered Sugar, facilitated this evolution, enabling Hayes to create music on his own terms and express his authentic self. These projects not only showcased Hayes' growth as an artist but also underscored his commitment to experimentation, collaboration, and emotional honesty. Through his independent endeavors, Hayes solidified his legacy as a visionary artist, inspiring countless others to pursue their creative passions with authenticity and courage.

Chapter 5: Later Career and Recent Works

Secret Codes and Battleships (2011)

Darren Hayes' 2011 album, Secret Codes and Battleships, represents a pivotal moment in his artistic evolution, building on the foundation laid by his previous works while introducing new sonic elements and themes. This album marked a return to the mainstream after his independent ventures and showcased Hayes' growth as a songwriter and musician. Secret Codes and Battleships encapsulates his journey of self-discovery, vulnerability, and emotional exploration, resonating with fans and critics alike.

Secret Codes and Battleships emerged during a transformative period in Hayes' life. After the success of his independent projects, Hayes sought to create an album that would bridge the gap between his past and present while exploring themes of love, loss, identity, and personal growth. The title itself reflects the duality of the human experience, with "secret codes" symbolizing the hidden emotions and complexities of relationships, while "battleships" evokes the struggles and conflicts inherent in love and self-discovery.

Throughout the album, Hayes delves into various facets of human connection, examining both the joys and sorrows that accompany intimacy. The lyrics are imbued with a sense of honesty and introspection, drawing from Hayes' own experiences and emotions. In interviews, Hayes emphasized his desire to create a deeply personal work that would resonate with listeners, allowing them to find solace and understanding in his music.

Key Themes

1. Love and Vulnerability: Hayes explores the intricacies of love and the vulnerability that accompanies it. Songs like "Talk Talk Talk" reflect the challenges of communication in relationships, while "Almost Lovers" captures the bittersweet nature of unfulfilled connections.

2. Self-Discovery and Growth: The album also emphasizes the journey of self-discovery, as Hayes reflects on his own identity and the experiences that have shaped him. Tracks like "Bloodstained Heart" and "You" convey the emotional complexity of self-acceptance and the quest for authenticity.

3. Conflict and Resolution: The juxtaposition of "secret codes" and "battleships" symbolizes the inner conflicts we face in relationships. Hayes tackles themes of misunderstandings and the struggle for resolution, allowing listeners to connect with their own experiences of love and heartache.

Musical Style and Production

Musically, Secret Codes and Battleships represents a synthesis of Hayes' earlier pop sensibilities with more contemporary electronic and alternative influences. The album showcases a diverse array of sounds, blending orchestral elements, synths, and rich instrumentation to create a layered and dynamic listening experience.

Influences and Collaborations

For the production of Secret Codes and Battleships, Hayes collaborated with renowned producers and musicians, including the likes of Stuart Crichton and Robert Conley, who played a pivotal role in shaping the album's sound. The partnership with Crichton, known for his work with various international artists, brought a fresh perspective to Hayes' music. This collaboration allowed Hayes to experiment with different production techniques, resulting in a modern sound that still retained his signature style.

The album features lush arrangements, incorporating strings, synths, and electronic beats to create a rich sonic landscape. Songs like "Crush" and "The Mirror" exemplify this blend of orchestral and electronic elements, showcasing Hayes' ability to fuse genres seamlessly. The production choices enhance the emotional depth of the lyrics, elevating the overall listening experience.

Standout Tracks

1. "Talk Talk Talk": The lead single from the album, "Talk Talk Talk," combines infectious pop melodies with introspective lyrics about communication and

connection in relationships. The upbeat production contrasts with the poignant themes, making it both a danceable track and a reflective piece.

2. "Bloodstained Heart": This song delves into the themes of love and loss, showcasing Hayes' vulnerability and emotional depth. The haunting melody, combined with powerful vocals, creates a poignant listening experience that resonates with listeners.

3. "You": A standout track that highlights Hayes' introspective lyricism and emotive vocal delivery. The song explores themes of self-discovery and acceptance, capturing the essence of personal growth and vulnerability.

Reception and Impact

Upon its release in 2011, Secret Codes and Battleships received a generally positive response from both fans and critics. Many praised Hayes for his artistic evolution and the emotional depth of the album, noting its introspective themes and sophisticated production. The album debuted at number one on the

Australian albums chart, reaffirming Hayes' status as a prominent figure in the music industry.

Critical Reception

Critics noted the album's departure from Hayes' earlier pop sound, acknowledging the more mature and introspective approach he took with Secret Codes and Battleships. The blend of electronic and orchestral elements was particularly highlighted, with many applauding the production choices that enhanced the emotional weight of the songs.

However, some reviews pointed out that the album's experimental nature might not appeal to all listeners, particularly those expecting a return to Hayes' more traditional pop sound. Nevertheless, the overall consensus was that Hayes had successfully navigated a new artistic direction while maintaining his core identity as a songwriter.

Fan Response and Legacy

Fans embraced Secret Codes and Battleships, resonating with its themes of vulnerability and self-exploration. The album became a source of comfort for many listeners, reflecting their own experiences of love and heartache. Hayes' ability to articulate complex emotions struck a chord with his audience, further solidifying his connection with them.

In retrospect, Secret Codes and Battleships is viewed as a significant work in Darren Hayes' discography. It encapsulates a critical phase in his career, marked by a return to the mainstream while retaining the authenticity and emotional depth that had defined his previous works. The album laid the groundwork for Hayes' subsequent projects, influencing his musical direction and creative choices in the years to come.

Darren Hayes' Secret Codes and Battleships stands as a testament to his artistic growth and commitment to exploring the complexities of the human experience. Through its themes of love, vulnerability, and self-discovery, the album resonates with listeners, inviting them to reflect on their own journeys. Hayes' ability to blend diverse musical influences and create emotionally resonant songs showcases his talent as a songwriter and musician. As

Hayes continues to evolve as an artist, Secret Codes and Battleships remains a defining moment in his career, highlighting his resilience and dedication to authenticity in music.

Homosexual (2022)

Darren Hayes' 2022 album, Homosexual, marks a significant and poignant chapter in his artistic journey, capturing his experiences as a queer individual and exploring themes of love, identity, and acceptance. This album is not just a collection of songs; it represents a deeply personal narrative that reflects Hayes' evolution as an artist and as a person. After years of navigating the complexities of fame, relationships, and self-acceptance, Homosexual serves as a celebration of his identity and a declaration of love in its many forms.

Homosexual is an album that embodies the essence of Darren Hayes' life experiences, particularly focusing on his journey of self-acceptance as a gay man. The title itself is a bold proclamation, stripping away stigma and embracing the beauty of LGBTQ+ identity. The album was created in the context of a world that is becoming increasingly accepting of diverse sexualities, yet still grapples with prejudice and misunderstanding. Hayes uses his platform to foster conversations around these themes, emphasizing the importance of love and acceptance.

Key Themes

1. Pride and Identity: One of the most prominent themes of the album is pride in one's identity. Hayes openly celebrates his sexuality, offering a refreshing perspective on being gay in a society that still has its challenges regarding acceptance. Songs like "Let It Go" and "Homosexual" embrace the notion of living authentically and unapologetically.

2. Love in Its Many Forms: The album explores the multifaceted nature of love, including romantic love, friendship, and self-love. Hayes delves into the complexities of relationships, addressing the joys and struggles of finding genuine connections. Tracks such as "All You Pretty Things" celebrate love and beauty in all its diversity.

3. Vulnerability and Healing: In Homosexual, Hayes reflects on vulnerability, emotional wounds, and the

healing process. The lyrics convey a sense of honesty and rawness, addressing the difficulties of past relationships while highlighting the importance of personal growth. The emotional depth of songs like "Love is Love" serves as an anthem for resilience and healing.

Musical Style and Production

Musically, Homosexual showcases a blend of pop, electronic, and orchestral elements, reflecting Hayes' diverse influences and his ability to create rich, layered soundscapes. The production is polished and contemporary, yet it retains an intimacy that allows listeners to connect deeply with the material.

Influences and Collaborations

Hayes collaborated with several talented producers and musicians to bring Homosexual to life. His long-time collaborator, Stuart Crichton, was instrumental in crafting the album's sound, utilizing a combination of electronic beats and orchestral arrangements. This partnership allowed Hayes to experiment with different sonic textures, resulting in a cohesive yet varied listening experience.

The album features a range of styles, from upbeat dance tracks to slower, more introspective ballads. This diversity reflects Hayes' ability to traverse genres while maintaining his signature pop sensibility.

Standout Tracks

1. "Homosexual": The title track is a bold and unapologetic anthem that encapsulates the spirit of the album. With infectious melodies and powerful lyrics, Hayes celebrates his identity while encouraging others to embrace their true selves. The chorus serves as a rallying cry for acceptance and love, making it a standout moment on the album.

2. "Let It Go": This track highlights the themes of self-acceptance and release. The song's uplifting message encourages listeners to let go of fear and embrace their identity, showcasing Hayes' talent for crafting emotionally resonant pop music.

3. "Love is Love": An anthemic celebration of love in all its forms, this song captures the essence of inclusivity. Its catchy chorus and vibrant production

make it a feel-good track that resonates with the LGBTQ+ community and allies alike.

Reception and Impact

Upon its release, Homosexual received widespread acclaim from fans and critics. Many praised Hayes for his courage in addressing themes of sexuality and identity while celebrating the beauty of love and acceptance. The album debuted at impressive chart positions, reaffirming Hayes' relevance in the contemporary music landscape.

Critical Reception

Critics lauded the album for its honest and open exploration of queer identity. Many noted Hayes' growth as a songwriter, highlighting the emotional depth and relatability of the lyrics. The combination of infectious melodies and poignant themes resonated with audiences, leading to discussions around LGBTQ+ representation in music.

Hayes' willingness to embrace his identity and share his experiences was seen as a powerful statement, inspiring many within the LGBTQ+ community. Critics emphasized the importance of visibility and representation, noting how Homosexual contributes to the ongoing conversation about acceptance and love.

Fan Response and Legacy

Fans embraced Homosexual as a celebration of love, identity, and self-acceptance. The album resonated deeply with those who have faced challenges related to their sexuality, providing a sense of hope and empowerment. Hayes' authenticity and vulnerability allowed listeners to connect with the material on a personal level, reinforcing his status as a beloved figure in the music industry.

The legacy of Homosexual extends beyond its musical impact. The album represents a cultural moment in which LGBTQ+ voices are becoming increasingly prominent in the mainstream. Hayes' openness about his identity encourages others to embrace their true selves, fostering a sense of community and solidarity among listeners.

Darren Hayes' Homosexual is more than just an album; it is a declaration of identity, love, and acceptance. Through its themes of pride, vulnerability, and emotional exploration, the album resonates with listeners, inviting them to reflect on their own journeys of self-discovery. Hayes' ability to blend diverse musical influences with deeply personal lyrics showcases his talent as an artist, reaffirming his place in the contemporary music landscape.

As society continues to evolve in its understanding of LGBTQ+ identities, Homosexual serves as a beacon of hope and celebration. Hayes' courage in addressing these themes allows for meaningful conversations around acceptance and love, making the album a significant contribution to both his discography and the broader cultural narrative. Ultimately, Homosexual stands as a testament to Darren Hayes' resilience, artistry, and unwavering commitment to authenticity.

Exploring New Sounds and Messages

Darren Hayes, renowned for his distinct voice and emotive songwriting, has continuously evolved as an artist, pushing the boundaries of pop music while embracing diverse influences and themes. As he has navigated his career from the iconic duo Savage Garden to his solo endeavors, Hayes has explored new sounds and messages that reflect both his personal experiences and the broader cultural landscape. This chapter delves into the ways Hayes has experimented with musical styles and lyrical content, emphasizing his journey of exploration and self-discovery.

Hayes' musical evolution is characterized by a willingness to embrace various genres and styles, resulting in a rich and diverse discography. Each phase of his career reflects a different aspect of his artistry, showcasing his ability to adapt and innovate.

Early Works: Pop and Beyond

Hayes' early work with Savage Garden established him as a pop icon, with hits like "I Want You" and "Truly Madly Deeply" showcasing his signature sound. However, even in these early years, hints of experimentation were evident. The duo's blend of pop, rock, and acoustic elements laid the foundation for Hayes' later exploration of diverse genres.

As a solo artist, Hayes began to venture into more varied musical landscapes. His debut album, Spin (2002), introduced elements of dance-pop and electronic music, reflecting the changing tides of the pop genre at the time. This willingness to incorporate new sounds demonstrated Hayes' desire to innovate while remaining true to his pop roots.

Embracing New Genres

As his career progressed, Hayes delved into different genres, expanding his musical palette. His albums, such as The Tension and the Spark (2004) and This Delicate Thing We've Made (2007), showcased a shift toward more experimental sounds, incorporating elements of rock, electronic, and orchestral music.

- The Tension and the Spark: This album marked a significant departure from traditional pop structures, featuring lush arrangements and introspective lyrics. Hayes experimented with production techniques, using atmospheric soundscapes to enhance the emotional depth of the music. The album's lead single, "Darkness," reflects this shift, combining haunting melodies with intricate electronic beats.

- This Delicate Thing We've Made: In this ambitious double album, Hayes pushed the boundaries even further, integrating various styles and influences. The work is characterized by a blend of orchestral arrangements, electronic elements, and personal storytelling. Songs like "On the Verge of Something Wonderful" and "Step into the Light" highlight his ability to fuse different musical genres while maintaining a cohesive narrative.

Lyrical Themes and Messages

Alongside his musical exploration, Hayes has consistently addressed meaningful themes and messages in his lyrics. His songwriting reflects a deep introspection, often drawing from personal experiences, relationships, and societal issues.

Identity and Self-Acceptance

As a gay artist navigating the complexities of identity, Hayes' lyrics often center on themes of self-acceptance and authenticity. His openness about his sexuality and personal struggles resonates with many listeners, providing a sense of comfort and validation.

- Honest Reflection: In songs like "I Can't Help You," Hayes confronts the challenges of vulnerability and emotional honesty. The lyrics delve into the intricacies of relationships, exploring the tension between desire and fear. This honest reflection allows listeners to connect with Hayes' experiences on a personal level.

- Celebration of Love: Hayes' music also celebrates love in its many forms, embracing both romantic and platonic connections. Tracks such as "Love is Love" and "Let It Go" emphasize the importance of love and acceptance, encouraging listeners to embrace their identities and relationships unapologetically.

Social Commentary

Hayes has used his platform to address broader societal issues, including LGBTQ+ rights, mental health, and the importance of compassion. His willingness to tackle these themes in his music reflects a commitment to using his voice for positive change.

- Advocacy and Awareness: In Homosexual (2022), Hayes directly confronts societal prejudices and celebrates LGBTQ+ identity. The album serves as an anthem for acceptance, with lyrics that challenge discrimination and promote love. Hayes' exploration of these themes not only resonates with the LGBTQ+ community but also encourages allies to engage in conversations around acceptance.

- Mental Health: Hayes' candidness about mental health struggles is evident in his lyrics. He often addresses feelings of anxiety, depression, and self-doubt, fostering discussions about mental well-being. By sharing his experiences, Hayes helps to destigmatize these issues, encouraging others to seek help and support.

The Impact of Exploration

Hayes' exploration of new sounds and messages has left a profound impact on both his music and his audience. His willingness to evolve as an artist has garnered him a dedicated fan base that appreciates his authenticity and vulnerability.

Connection with Fans

Fans have responded positively to Hayes' artistic evolution, recognizing the depth and sincerity in his work. His willingness to share his personal journey has fostered a sense of community among listeners, many of whom find solace and inspiration in his music.

- Engagement and Support: Through social media and live performances, Hayes has cultivated a strong connection with his audience. His openness invites fans to share their own experiences, creating a space for dialogue and support. This engagement reinforces the idea that music can be a powerful tool for healing and connection.

Influence on Contemporary Music

Hayes' exploration of diverse sounds and themes has influenced contemporary pop music, inspiring a new generation of artists to embrace authenticity and vulnerability in their work. His ability to blend genres and address complex issues in his lyrics has paved the way for artists who seek to break free from traditional pop conventions.

- Encouraging Diversity: Hayes' willingness to challenge norms has encouraged other artists to experiment with their sound and explore meaningful themes. As a result, the pop landscape has become increasingly diverse, with artists drawing from a range of influences and backgrounds.

Darren Hayes' journey of exploring new sounds and messages reflects his growth as an artist and a person. Through his willingness to experiment with musical styles and address meaningful themes, Hayes has created a body of work that resonates deeply with his audience.

His evolution serves as a testament to the power of authenticity and vulnerability in music, encouraging listeners to embrace their identities and engage in conversations about love, acceptance, and mental health. As Hayes continues to navigate his artistic path, his exploration of new sounds and messages will undoubtedly leave a lasting impact on the music industry and inspire future generations of artists In doing so, Hayes cements his legacy as a pioneering figure in contemporary pop music, championing the values of love, acceptance, and self-discovery.

Chapter 6: Notable Singles and Music Videos

Darren Hayes has established himself as a prominent figure in the music industry, not only for his impressive vocal abilities and songwriting talents but also for his innovative approach to visual storytelling through music videos. This chapter explores Hayes' notable singles as a solo artist, the artistic vision behind his music videos, and his collaborations with other artists that have further enriched his musical journey.

Hit Singles as a Solo Artist

Darren Hayes' transition from the success of Savage Garden to a solo career was marked by several hit singles that solidified his place in the music industry. Each single reflects his growth as an artist, showcasing his ability to craft compelling melodies, poignant lyrics, and memorable hooks.

"Insatiable" (2004)

As the lead single from his debut solo album Spin, "Insatiable" became one of Hayes' most iconic songs. The lush arrangement and romantic lyrics illustrate the intensity of desire and love. The song's success, reaching the top 10 in several countries, established Hayes as a formidable solo artist, capable of creating emotionally charged pop ballads.

"So Beautiful" (2004)

"So Beautiful" further showcased Hayes' skill for crafting heartfelt ballads. With simple yet evocative piano arrangements and lyrics celebrating love, the song resonated deeply with fans. Its chart success and widespread acclaim contributed to Hayes' reputation as a masterful storyteller.

"Strange Relationship" (2004)

Following the success of "Insatiable," "Strange Relationship" demonstrated Hayes' versatility in blending upbeat pop elements with introspective lyrics. The catchy chorus and engaging melodies helped the track achieve chart success, further establishing his solo career.

"Power of Love" (2005)

Hayes' rendition of "The Power of Love" highlighted his vocal prowess and emotional depth. The orchestral arrangement and heartfelt lyrics resonated with audiences, achieving top-chart positions and reinforcing his ability to reinterpret classic songs in a contemporary context.

"Listen All You People" (2007)

From the ambitious double album This Delicate Thing We've Made, "Listen All You People" featured an experimental sound that incorporated electronic elements. The track's introspective lyrics and innovative production demonstrated Hayes' willingness to evolve artistically, even if it meant departing from mainstream pop conventions.

"Talk Talk Talk" (2011)

With its upbeat tempo and catchy chorus, "Talk Talk Talk" marked a return to pop sensibilities for Hayes in his album Secret Codes and Battleships. The lyrics emphasized the importance of communication in relationships, while the infectious melody ensured it became a fan favorite.

"Homosexual" (2022)

Hayes' recent single "Homosexual" exemplifies his growth as an artist and advocate for the LGBTQ+ community. With empowering lyrics and a catchy melody, the track celebrates love and acceptance, reinforcing Hayes' commitment to authenticity and inclusivity.

Visual Storytelling in Darren Hayes' Music Videos

In addition to his successful singles, Darren Hayes has produced a series of visually striking music videos that enhance the narratives of his songs. Each video serves as an extension of his artistic vision, incorporating elements of storytelling, emotion, and aesthetics to create a profound viewer experience.

"Insatiable" (2004)

The music video for "Insatiable" features a cinematic approach that mirrors the song's themes of longing and desire. Shot in a moody, atmospheric style, the video includes intimate and passionate imagery, reflecting the emotional depth of the lyrics. Hayes' performance is both vulnerable and captivating, allowing viewers to connect with the song on a personal level.

"So Beautiful" (2004)

In "So Beautiful," the music video captures the essence of the song's celebration of love. The visuals are simple yet effective, featuring intimate moments between couples and showcasing the beauty of love in various forms. The soft lighting and warm tones create an inviting atmosphere that complements the song's heartfelt lyrics, further enhancing its impact.

"Strange Relationship" (2004)

The video for "Strange Relationship" adopts a more dynamic visual style, incorporating fast cuts and vivid imagery that reflect the song's upbeat tempo. The juxtaposition of light and shadow symbolizes the complexities of romantic relationships, while Hayes' charismatic performance adds a layer of energy to the visual narrative.

"Power of Love" (2005)

Hayes' video for "The Power of Love" is a visually stunning interpretation of the song's themes of devotion and commitment. The use of dramatic lighting and powerful imagery elevates the emotional stakes, emphasizing the song's romantic undertones. Hayes' passionate performance further captivates viewers, showcasing his vocal strength and stage presence.

"Listen All You People" (2007)

The music video for "Listen All You People" features a more abstract visual style, complementing the experimental nature of the song. Surreal imagery and innovative editing techniques create a dreamlike atmosphere that enhances the themes of communication and connection. Hayes' performance is introspective, inviting viewers to engage with the deeper meaning behind the lyrics.

"Talk Talk Talk" (2011)

In the video for "Talk Talk Talk," Hayes presents a vibrant and colorful visual experience that mirrors the song's upbeat message. The energetic choreography and lively settings create a sense of joy and connection, emphasizing the importance of open communication in relationships. The visuals reflect Hayes' commitment to crafting engaging and meaningful narratives through his music.

"Homosexual" (2022)

The music video for "Homosexual" is a bold and unapologetic celebration of LGBTQ+ identity. Featuring vibrant colors and powerful imagery, the video portrays love in all its forms, emphasizing the importance of self-acceptance and empowerment. Hayes' authentic portrayal of himself and his message resonates deeply with viewers, making it a significant visual statement in his career.

Collaborations and Features with Other Artists

Throughout his career, Darren Hayes has collaborated with a variety of artists, further enriching his musical repertoire. These collaborations highlight his versatility as a vocalist and songwriter, allowing him to explore new sounds and creative directions.

Collaboration with Savage Garden

While Hayes is primarily known for his solo work, his collaboration with Savage Garden co-member Daniel Jones remains significant. The duo's chemistry and shared vision created a string of hits that defined the late 1990s and early 2000s. Songs like "Truly Madly Deeply" and "I Knew I Loved You" showcased their unique sound, and while these are not solo efforts, they laid the groundwork for Hayes' future collaborations.

"Creep" (with Mondo) (2010)

In 2010, Hayes collaborated with the electronic duo Mondo on their rendition of "Creep," originally by Radiohead. This cover showcased Hayes' ability to adapt to different musical styles while retaining his signature vocal flair. The collaboration received positive reviews, illustrating Hayes' versatility and willingness to explore new genres.

"I Can't Help You" (with David Archuleta) (2012)
Hayes joined forces with American Idol finalist David Archuleta on the duet "I Can't Help You." The song features harmonious vocals and heartfelt lyrics, highlighting the emotional connection between the two artists. Their collaboration received praise for its sincerity and melodic beauty, further emphasizing Hayes' ability to connect with fellow artists.

"Put It On Me" (with DJ A1) (2020)
In 2020, Hayes collaborated with DJ A1 on the single "Put It On Me." This track marked a departure from his previous work, incorporating electronic elements and a contemporary sound. The collaboration

showcased Hayes' willingness to experiment with different styles while maintaining his artistic integrity.

"We Are Smug" (with Chris and James) (2018)

Hayes collaborated with Chris and James on the album "We Are Smug, which features a collection of songs that blend their distinct sounds. The collaboration reflects Hayes' artistic evolution and willingness to explore new creative avenues, demonstrating his commitment to pushing the boundaries of pop music.

Darren Hayes' notable singles and music videos reflect his remarkable journey as a solo artist. Each single showcases his ability to craft emotionally resonant songs while his music videos serve as powerful visual narratives that enhance the themes of his work. Through collaborations with other artists, Hayes continues to evolve and innovate, enriching his musical repertoire and further solidifying his place in the music industry. As he continues to create, his contributions to pop music and visual storytelling remain significant, inspiring fans and fellow artists alike.

Chapter 7: Darren Hayes' Legacy and Impact

Darren Hayes' career is marked by significant commercial success, characterized by impressive sales figures, chart-topping singles, and numerous accolades. This chapter delves into the metrics that define Hayes' achievements as a solo artist, showcasing his impact on the music industry and his enduring appeal to audiences worldwide.

Album Sales and Chart Performance

From the outset of his solo career, Darren Hayes has enjoyed considerable success on the charts, both in his home country of Australia and internationally. His albums and singles have consistently resonated with listeners, resulting in impressive sales figures and chart placements.

"Spin" (2002)

Hayes' debut solo album, Spin, released in 2002, marked a pivotal moment in his career. The album debuted at number one on the Australian Albums Chart, achieving multi-platinum status. With hit singles such as "Insatiable" and "So Beautiful," Spin sold over 1 million copies worldwide. The album's commercial success established Hayes as a formidable solo artist following his tenure with Savage Garden.

"The Tension and the Spark" (2004)
The follow-up album, The Tension and the Spark, was released in 2004 and reached the top 10 in Australia, achieving gold certification. The album featured hit singles like "Darkness" and "Pop!Ular SciencE," both of which contributed to the album's overall success. While it did not achieve the same level of commercial success as Spin, it solidified Hayes' reputation as an artist willing to take creative risks.

This Delicate Thing We've Made (2007)
Hayes' ambitious double album, This Delicate Thing We've Made, was released in 2007 and debuted at

number 8 on the Australian Albums Chart. The album was well-received by critics and fans alike, showcasing Hayes' artistic evolution. While it did not achieve multi-platinum status, it sold over 100,000 copies in Australia and generated notable singles like "On the Verge of Something Wonderful."

Secret Codes and Battleships (2011)

With Secret Codes and Battleships, released in 2011, Hayes returned to a more mainstream sound. The album debuted at number 5 on the ARIA Charts and was met with positive reviews. Featuring the hit single "Talk Talk Talk," the album continued to build on Hayes' legacy, selling over 50,000 copies in Australia and receiving gold certification.

Homosexual (2022)

Hayes' recent album, Homosexual, released in 2022, marked a significant moment in his career. The album debuted at number 3 on the Australian Albums Chart, reflecting a resurgence in Hayes' popularity. It was particularly notable for its themes of love and acceptance, resonating with both fans and critics. The album's success indicated Hayes' continued relevance in the ever-evolving music landscape.

Darren Hayes' chart achievements are a testament to his enduring popularity and musical prowess. His ability to connect with audiences has led to numerous chart-topping hits and a series of notable achievements throughout his career.

Singles Chart Performance

Several of Hayes' singles have reached impressive positions on various charts, both in Australia and internationally. "Insatiable," for example, peaked at number 5 on the Australian Singles Chart and achieved success in other countries, including the UK and the US.

"So Beautiful," another hit single from Spin, reached number 1 on the Australian Singles Chart and garnered significant airplay, further cementing Hayes' status as a solo artist. Similarly, "Strange Relationship" reached the top 10 in Australia, showcasing Hayes' ability to produce commercially successful singles.

In addition to his chart success, Hayes has had multiple entries on the Billboard charts in the United States, including the Billboard Hot 100 and the Billboard Adult Contemporary Chart. His international presence has helped broaden his fan base and establish him as a respected artist in the global music scene.

Awards and Nominations

Darren Hayes' commercial success has been recognized through numerous awards and nominations, reflecting his impact on the music industry. Over the years, he has received accolades for his songwriting, vocal performance, and artistic contributions.

- ARIA Awards: Hayes has been nominated for several Australian Recording Industry Association (ARIA) Awards, including wins for Best Pop Release and Best Single for "Truly Madly Deeply" with Savage Garden. His solo work has also garnered nominations for Best Male Artist and Best Pop Album.

- MTV Australia Video Music Awards: Hayes has been recognized at the MTV Australia Video Music Awards, with nominations for Best Male Artist and Best Pop Video, showcasing his appeal to younger audiences and his innovative approach to music videos.

Australian Music Prize: Hayes was nominated for the Australian Music Prize for his album This Delicate Thing We've Made, reflecting critical acclaim for his work as a solo artist.

- International Recognition: Beyond Australia, Hayes has received international recognition, including nominations at the International Dance Music Awards and the World Music Awards, showcasing his global appeal.

Influence on Pop Music and Legacy

Darren Hayes' commercial success extends beyond mere sales figures and awards; it encompasses his influence on pop music and his enduring legacy as an artist. His ability to blend genres, explore personal themes, and connect with audiences has set him apart in the music industry.

Innovation in Songwriting

Hayes is celebrated for his innovative approach to songwriting, often exploring themes of love, identity, and emotional depth. His willingness to experiment with different musical styles and production techniques has influenced a new generation of artists, encouraging them to push boundaries and embrace their authenticity.

Advocacy for LGBTQ+ Rights

As an openly gay artist, Hayes has been a vocal advocate for LGBTQ+ rights and representation within the music industry. His songs often reflect themes of acceptance, love, and self-discovery, resonating with audiences who seek authentic representation in popular culture. His recent album Homosexual is a testament to his commitment to advocating for equality and celebrating love in all its forms.

Impact on Future Artists

Hayes' commercial success and artistic contributions have inspired countless aspiring musicians. His ability to transition from a successful group to a solo career serves as a model for artists seeking to establish their identities and create meaningful connections with their audiences.

Darren Hayes' commercial success is defined by remarkable album sales, chart achievements, and significant awards throughout his career. His influence on pop music, combined with his advocacy for LGBTQ+ rights and innovative songwriting, has solidified his legacy as a groundbreaking artist. As Hayes continues to evolve and create, his impact on the music industry will undoubtedly resonate for generations to come.

Future Prospects and Continuing Musical Journey

As Darren Hayes continues to navigate his musical journey, the future appears bright, characterized by ongoing creativity, exploration of new sounds, and a commitment to personal and artistic growth. With a career spanning over two decades, Hayes has proven himself to be a resilient artist capable of adapting to changing musical landscapes while remaining true to his unique voice and vision. This chapter delves into the potential directions of Hayes' career, his artistic ambitions, and the impact he may have on the music industry in the years to come.

One of the hallmarks of Darren Hayes' career is his willingness to embrace change and experimentation. Each album he has released reflects a different chapter in his artistic evolution, showcasing his growth as a songwriter and performer.

Expanding Musical Horizons

With his recent album Homosexual, Hayes has demonstrated an eagerness to explore themes of love, acceptance, and identity. The critical acclaim and commercial success of the album indicate that fans appreciate his willingness to tackle complex emotions and societal issues through his music.

In the future, Hayes may continue to explore different genres, potentially incorporating elements of electronic music, indie pop, or even world music influences. As he has shown in the past, he has the ability to blend various styles, creating a sound that is distinctly his own while remaining fresh and relevant.

Collaborations and Innovations

The potential for collaborations with other artists presents an exciting avenue for Hayes. Over the years, he has worked with various musicians, and these collaborations have often resulted in unique and innovative sounds. By partnering with both established and emerging artists, Hayes can infuse his music with new perspectives and influences.

Given the rise of platforms like TikTok and Spotify, Hayes has the opportunity to reach new audiences and experiment with shorter formats, such as singles or EPs. This could allow him to respond to trends and engage with fans in real-time, fostering a sense of community around his music.

As an artist who has openly embraced his identity and advocated for LGBTQ+ rights, Hayes' journey is not just musical but also deeply personal. His commitment to advocacy and self-expression is likely to continue shaping his work and public persona.

Themes of Identity and Acceptance

The themes present in Homosexual highlight Hayes' desire to promote acceptance and understanding within society. In future projects, he may delve even deeper into these themes, exploring the nuances of identity and the complexities of love. By sharing his personal experiences, Hayes can create a safe space for listeners who resonate with his journey.

Hayes may also use his platform to speak on issues that affect marginalized communities, utilizing his influence to raise awareness and promote social change. His authenticity and vulnerability can inspire others to embrace their identities and advocate for acceptance and equality.

Mental Health and Well-being

The ongoing conversation about mental health in the music industry presents another opportunity for Hayes to contribute meaningfully. As artists increasingly open up about their struggles, Hayes can share his experiences and insights, encouraging discussions around mental health and well-being.

This could manifest in his music, through lyrics that address mental health challenges, or in other forms, such as interviews, social media engagement, or collaborations with mental health organizations. By prioritizing mental health advocacy, Hayes can foster a supportive environment for fans and fellow artists alike.

The relationship between an artist and their audience is crucial for sustaining a successful career. Hayes has cultivated a loyal fan base, and as he continues his journey, engaging with this community will be vital.

Utilizing Social Media Platforms

Hayes has effectively utilized social media platforms to connect with fans, sharing personal insights, behind-the-scenes content, and updates about his music. As these platforms evolve, he can explore new ways to engage with his audience, such as live streams, Q&A sessions, or exclusive content. This direct interaction fosters a sense of community, allowing fans to feel connected to Hayes as an individual rather than just an artist. Building this relationship can enhance their investment in his music, resulting in increased support for his future projects.

Fan-Driven Initiatives

Hayes might consider initiatives that allow fans to participate in his creative process. This could involve soliciting fan input on themes, artwork, or even song lyrics. By involving his audience in his work, Hayes can create a more collaborative environment that resonates with his supporters.

Darren Hayes has already made a significant impact on the music industry, and as he moves forward, his legacy will only grow. His contributions to pop music, advocacy for LGBTQ+ rights, and commitment to artistic integrity position him as a role model for aspiring musicians.

Influencing Future Generations

As an established artist, Hayes has the opportunity to mentor and inspire upcoming musicians. By sharing his experiences, insights, and lessons learned throughout his career, he can provide valuable guidance to those navigating the complexities of the music industry.

Hayes may also participate in workshops, panels, or industry events where he can share his knowledge and advocate for inclusivity and diversity in the arts. His influence can help pave the way for future generations of artists, ensuring that diverse voices are heard and celebrated.

A Lasting Artistic Legacy

Ultimately, Darren Hayes' future prospects are intertwined with his past achievements and his unwavering dedication to his craft. As he continues to evolve as an artist, his legacy will be defined not only by his commercial success but also by the meaningful connections he fosters with his audience and the impact he has on the music industry as a whole.

Darren Hayes' journey is a testament to the power of creativity, resilience, and self-expression. As he looks to the future, his artistic evolution, advocacy for acceptance, and engagement with fans will continue to shape his career. With a legacy built on authenticity and a commitment to pushing boundaries, Hayes is poised to make a lasting impact in the music industry, inspiring both current and future generations of artists.

Conclusion

The journey of Darren Hayes is one marked by resilience, creativity, and a profound commitment to authenticity. From his early days in Brisbane, Australia, to his rise as a global pop sensation with the iconic duo Savage Garden, Hayes has continually evolved as an artist, embracing both personal and musical transformations. His journey reflects not only his artistic aspirations but also his dedication to championing individuality and self-expression, particularly within the LGBTQ+ community.

Throughout this book, we have explored the various facets of Hayes' career, beginning with his formative years and early musical influences that laid the groundwork for his passion for music. The formation and subsequent success of Savage Garden showcased his remarkable talent and the profound impact of their chart-topping hits. This chapter of his life solidified Hayes' status in the music industry, leading to an inevitable transition into a solo career that would further challenge and define his artistic identity.

His solo debut with Spin introduced audiences to a new dimension of his artistry, highlighting a musical shift that was both experimental and introspective. The critical reception and chart success of this album set the stage for Hayes to explore deeper themes and soundscapes, culminating in his later works, such as The Tension and the Spark, where he unabashedly examined complex emotions and societal issues. Each subsequent album, including This Delicate Thing We've Made and Secret Codes and Battleships, marked significant milestones in his creative evolution, revealing a willingness to push boundaries and redefine his artistic direction.

Darren Hayes' journey is not solely defined by his music; it is also characterized by his unwavering advocacy for acceptance and love. His openness about his identity has provided a platform for others to find their voices, contributing to a broader dialogue on LGBTQ+ issues and mental health awareness. His recent album, Homosexual, is a celebration of self-acceptance and love, a culmination of his experiences and a beacon of hope for many.

As we consider the future prospects for Hayes, it is evident that his artistic journey is far from over. His embrace of new sounds and messages reflects a continuous evolution that resonates with fans and newcomers alike. The potential for collaboration, exploration of diverse genres, and engagement with his audience through innovative platforms presents exciting opportunities for Hayes to further his impact on the music landscape.

Moreover, Darren Hayes' legacy extends beyond his discography; it encompasses the meaningful connections he has cultivated with fans and the inspiration he provides to emerging artists. By mentoring the next generation of musicians and advocating for inclusivity within the industry, Hayes ensures that his influence will continue to reverberate for years to come.

In conclusion, Darren Hayes is not just a pop icon; he is a storyteller, an advocate, and a symbol of courage and authenticity in the music world. His journey is a testament to the power of self-expression and the importance of embracing one's true self. As he continues to create, inspire, and connect with his audience, there is no doubt that Darren Hayes will leave an indelible mark on the hearts of fans and the fabric of the music industry, solidifying his place as one of the most significant artists of our time.

Made in the USA
Columbia, SC
02 December 2024